AF414219

Title: Kids' Prayers for A Successful school Year: Kim Ruff Moore Publisher: Ruff Moore Media Publishing Publication Year: 2024 Illustrations: Kim Ruff Moore Book Cover: Kim Ruff Moore Printed in the United States of America
For permissions, please contact: Ruff Moore Media Publishing
ISBN 979-8-8693-8901-5
www.ruffmooremedia.com
www.kimruffmoore.com

May this book serve as a beacon of hope and inspiration for all children- guiding them towards a path of success, growth, and spiritual fulfillment in school and beyond.

Welcome to "Kids' Prayers for A Successful School Year" by Kim Ruff Moore. This book is a special companion for young learners embarking on the adventure of education. Within these pages, children will find a collection of prayers crafted to support them through the joys and challenges of school life.

As a Christian author, I understand the significance of faith and encouragement in a child's academic journey. With this in mind, have created this prayer guide to offer children a source of comfort, strength, and guidance as they navigate the exciting world of learning.

Each prayer in this guide addresses a specific aspect of school life, from wisdom and focus to friendship and perseverance. Whether seeking divine assistance before a test, asking for courage to speak up in class, or simply expressing gratitude for the gift of education, these prayers are meant to uplift young hearts and remind children that they are never alone on their educational journey.

Accompanied by colorful illustrations and heartfelt words, "A Child's Prayer Guide for Success in School" invites children to connect with God in a meaningful way, fostering a sense of peace, confidence, and resilience in the face of academic challenges.

Kids' Prayers for A Successful School Year
by Kim Ruff Moore

Gratitude:
Dear God,
First, I want to thank You for the opportunity to go to school. Not everyone gets this chance, and I'm truly grateful for it.
Bless me today at school- In the name of Jesus. Amen

Wisdom:

Please grant me wisdom, dear God. Help me to understand the lessons taught by my teachers and to apply them in my studies. Guide me in finding creative solutions to problems and in thinking critically. Bless me God- In the name of Jesus. Amen

Focus:
Dear God,
Sometimes, my mind wanders, and I find it hard to concentrate. Please help me to focus during class and while doing my homework. Remove any distractions that might keep me from learning. Bless me God.
In the name of Jesus.
Amen

Courage:

Dear God,

There are times when schoolwork seems difficult, and I feel scared or unsure. Give me courage, Lord, to face challenges head-on and to persevere even when things get tough.

Bless me God- In the name of Jesus. Amen

Patience:

Dear God,
Help me to be patient
with myself when I
don't understand
something right away.
Teach me to keep
trying and not to give
up easily. Bless me
God- In the name of
Jesus. Amen

Kindness:

Dear God,
May I always be kind to my classmates and teachers. Help me to offer help to those in need and to treat others with respect and understanding. Bless me God- In the name of Jesus. Amen

Responsibility:
Dear God,
Please help me to take responsibility for my actions, whether it's completing my assignments on time, being honest in my work, or taking care of my belongings. Bless me God- In the name of Jesus. Amen

Organization:

Dear God ,
Guide me in keeping my school materials and schedule organized. Help me to use my time wisely and to prioritize my tasks effectively. Bless me God- In the name of Jesus. Amen

Confidence:

Dear God,
Sometimes, I feel nervous, especially when speaking in front of the class or tackling a new subject. Please fill me with confidence, Lord, and remind me that You are always with me. Bless me God- In the name of Jesus. Amen

Friendship:

Dear God,
Bless me with good friends who support me and encourage me to do my best. Help me to be a good friend in return, offering help and kindness whenever I can. Bless me God- In the name of Jesus.
Amen

Health:

Dear God,
please keep me healthy so that I can attend school regularly and give my best effort in my studies. Bless me God- In the name of Jesus. Amen

Joy:

Dear God,
I ask for your joy to fill my heart each day at school. Help me to find joy in learning, in making new discoveries, and in the friendships I form.
Bless me God- In the name of Jesus. Amen

Thank you God for listening to my prayers. I trust in your guidance and love as I journey through my school days. Amen.

Epilogue
As you come to the end of this book, I hope you feel inspired and empowered to face the challenges and joys of school with courage, kindness, and perseverance. Remember, success in school is not just about getting good grades or achieving academic milestones, but also about growing as a person, making friends, and discovering your passions.
In these pages, you've found prayers to guide you through tests, friendships, challenges, and triumphs. May these prayers remind you that you are never alone, that you are loved, and that you have the strength within you to overcome any obstacle.
As you continue your journey through school and life, may you always hold onto the values of kindness, respect, and determination. Cherish the friendships you make along the way, and never forget to dream big and reach for the stars.

Meet the Author

Kim Ruff Moore is a multifaceted artist whose talents have touched hearts across the globe. As a Stellar Award-winning singer-songwriter and national recording artist, Kim's voice carries messages of hope and inspiration.

Beyond her musical achievements, Kim has established herself as a prolific author with an impressive repertoire of 35 published books. Her works span various genres, from children's literature to insightful guides on finances and relationships. Kim's dedication to uplifting others is evident in the five-star ratings her books consistently receive.

A champion of literacy, Kim has created several beloved book series for children, including "Suzzie Moch," "Spence Seven," "Sergio the Studio Mouse," "Kirby the Koala," and "Harper Sharper," among others. Through imaginative storytelling, Kim instills valuable lessons and fosters creativity in young minds.

Kim's creative endeavors extend beyond the written word. She is a proud member of the duo group "The New Consolers," alongside her husband, Jeffrey Moore, who is a renowned music producer with roots in the legendary Sam Cooke band. Jeffrey's induction into the DooWap Hall of Fame in 2013 is a testament to his musical legacy. Together, Kim and Jeffrey captivate audiences worldwide with their soul-stirring performances. Their shared passion for music and storytelling creates an unforgettable experience for listeners of all ages.

In addition to her artistic pursuits, Kim generously shares her literary platform at various functions and speaking engagements, inspiring others to pursue their passions and fulfill their potential.

Kim and Jeffrey's family life is equally enriching, with four children who undoubtedly inherit their parents' creativity and drive. Their son Spencer, also a writer, serves as the inspiration behind the acclaimed "Spence Seven" book series, continuing the family's legacy of storytelling and inspiration.

Through her music, writing, and advocacy, Kim Ruff Moore continues to make a profound impact, spreading joy and empowerment wherever her talents take her.